Cooking

with Dat

NEW ORLEANS
Love

TRINESE DUPLESSIS

ISBN: 979-8-218-22888-0 (Paperback)
ISBN: 978-1-0881-7291-9 (ePub)

I dedicate this recipe book to God, the Supreme Being, my Lord and Savior Jesus Christ, my Grandmother Lois Knox Finley, and my elders who cooked all those beautiful meals throughout my lifetime. My Grandmother Lois is the reason I learned to master the skills of cooking with love. I was in the kitchen with her at the tender age of three years old. She is the reason I love fresh seasoning, herbs, and cooking meals from scratch.

I especially dedicate this book to my amazing, beautiful, and gifted son, *Gentle Giant* who towers over me, Orion E. Duplessis, and his future children. I want to leave a legacy, a blueprint behind for them to learn and enjoy the fruits of my labor. Bonding with God and family through cooking is important to me.

Acknowledgments

I must thank my beautiful husband, Orion G. Duplessis, for always pushing and motivating me to do my best for 30-plus years. He has always supported me 150% and brought out many of my gifts and talents, including the establishment of my catering business *Oritri Catering*. The meaning of it comes from the first three letters of our names. When you have a strong support system from your spouse, the sky is the limit.

I want to thank my family, supporters, clients, friends, strangers, fellow chefs, artists, and businesses that have allowed me to create masterpiece dishes for the masses. This has been one very blessed journey and God is not through…it's only upward from here.

Bible Scripture: Jeremiah 29:11 (NIV) "For I know the plans I have for you, "declares the Lord, "plans to prosper you and not to harm you, plans to give you hope and a future."

Contents

Jaw-dropping Soups, Gumbo, Fish

Mouth Watering Desserts

Introduction

I was born and raised in New Orleans, Louisiana, in 1973. My beautiful mother, Terri Finely, had my sister Keyanna Jordan and me, with my father Roy Duplessis. My father lived just around the corner with my late grandparents Mervin and Mae Duplessis, who had 11 children. My mother, my sister, and I lived with our grandparents (my mother's parents), Henry, also known as Grady, and Lois Finley who had 5 children. We lived there for the first five years of my life. When my mother married my late stepfather, Morris Jordan Jr., in 1978, we had two more siblings added to our family, Morris Jordan III, and Michael Jordan. We moved next door to my new set of amazing grandparents, the late Morris Jordan Sr. and Bernice Jordan. They are the reason my sister and I got baptized. My beautiful grandparents, my mother's parents, the late Henry Grady Finley, and Lois Finely who is still living, were from a small town called Utica, Mississippi. They both came from very large families. They fell in love and got married and moved to New Orleans around 1955. My grandfather Grady found work as a truck driver and worked for a company for 40 years. After he retired, he was awarded for driving over 2 million miles.

My grandmother was a homemaker, and she would light up the kitchen every day with hot meals, although my Grandfather Grady would be on the road truck driving. She still had mouths to feed and was thrilled to manage the household. In fact, she just did pretty much everything with five children and two grandchildren. Yet, when my grandfather was on the road, he expected her to cook wonderful meals; he loved her cooking. His mouth would literally drool every time he was about to partake of one of her delectable creations. It was a sight to see all of us waiting to eat her cooking. I remember at three years old watching my grandmother cut up fresh seasoning by hand. No machines, she did everything with a knife. This was the start of my culinary journey and cooking lessons. It was always bonding and family time in the kitchen. One time my grandfather brought home rabbit meat, and he tricked me and told me it was roast. Lord have mercy, it was so good! After I ate a plateful and licked the gravy, he told me that I had just eaten rabbit. I think I cried for like two seconds and said, "*That rabbit was good, I want some more.*"

My grandmother Lois is the oldest of ten children. She started cooking very young. At about 8 years old, she was helping my great-grandmother Ada Knox (Madea) with the meals for the family. When the other siblings got older, especially all her sisters, they learned to cook too.

I come from a long line of gifted cooks and bakers. In those days, families had farms on their own property. Chickens, okra, snap beans, vegetables, fresh herbs, etc., were raised right on that Mississippi land. Imagine every year when we had family reunions, how many people were in our families, and how much Southern food was cooked for us. Everyone cooked everything from scratch, and no one went hungry. It was a blessing to experience that.

My mother told us stories about how every summer as a child she and my uncles would go to Mississippi, and how much they enjoyed being with both sets of my great-grandparents. She said that everything was grown on the land, okra, several types of fruits (peaches, plums, watermelons), snap peas, and black-eyed peas, and they would eat and help pick them. She also said they would tend to the chickens, pigs, and cows. It was exciting and therapeutic. Freshly grown food kept our elders and relatives living long lives. My late great-grandpa Johnny Finley, my grandpa Henry Grady (Finley's son), lived well past his 90s, and I remember how funny he was. He was a real jokester.

My grandmother brought her Southern cooking skills and mastered the New Orleans soul creole food and Cajun dishes. I swear I don't know who taught her, but if you didn't know any better, you would have thought she was born and raised in New Orleans. My grandmother fed everyone in the neighborhood. Her home was like an open restaurant. You could smell the food a mile away. She was affectionately known by everyone as the Gumbo Queen. She was that and so much more. She cooked the most tasteful and fulfilling gumbo ever, with huge quantities of seafood and meat. The pot was huge, and the roux was so perfect and thick. No one in the family ever cooked gumbo but her, until I started some years ago. The peculiar thing was she only cooked it twice a year on Christmas and Thanksgiving. A funny incident, one of our cousins on my grandfather's side, would visit every Sunday for years, he literally would fix a huge plate, put it in the car, and fix another huge plate to eat. He did not know we all knew he did that. I have countless stories of people coming from all around, taking plates of food home, and she never stopped them. She has a big heart and just loved cooking and making others happy with her meals. No one went hungry. For more than 35 years some of our Mississippi family members would come to New Orleans for the holidays, especially Thanksgiving, and get in that kitchen and cook so much food it was crazy. I learned how to cook in a loving atmosphere. I cooked and watched the elders cook with so much love. They could put so many modern restaurants out of business with their authentic Southern cooking. It was a blessing to experience all of this, especially in a close-knit family. My grandmother loved having a house full of people.

God trained my grandmother and she and God trained me. After my beloved grandfather Henry Grady Finley died in 2015, life changed for us all. He was the biggest comedian ever and would outlaugh all of us with his own jokes. He adored my grandmother and her cooking. I remember his huge bowls of gumbo and his plates would be so full, especially for the holidays. Even after his death, she still cooked until about 2018. I started Oritri Catering that same year. Everything I learned from my elders is now being used in my kitchen. I started cooking her famous gumbo utilizing her authentic recipe, and then I made my recipe, a dry powdered roux, and combined the two together and it is a hit. God is so good. When the pandemic hit in 2020, I left my 9 to 5 job of 14 years to pursue catering full-time. I also started a cooking show called "Cooking with Love," and the rest is history. It's nothing like sharing love from your kitchen with the people you love!

Meaning of the Holy Trinity

Many cooks, chefs, mothers, fathers, and families used this method to cook Cajun, and creole soul food dishes in Louisiana. It consists of the tear-jerking onion, bell pepper, and celery. Sometimes that is all you had to cook with, and again it's fresh seasoning. You will soon find out that I am not a celery lover at all. But I will use bell peppers and onions often in many of my recipes. Celery has a bold taste, and you don't want to use too much, as it can overpower other seasonings.

Creole Orleans Mirliton Dressing, Creamy Creole Potato Salad with Corn

Deep South New Orleans Seafood Recipes

Feisty Seafood Stuffed Bell Peppers

My grandmother loved cooking bell peppers, and she often used ground meat in hers. Stuffed bell peppers are a big tradition in New Orleans. You cook them for every holiday, and it would be a crime if you didn't. My grandmother would cook so many bell peppers! I just couldn't understand how, but then I found out. She would cook and freeze them for later, and she stayed on top of her game. But baby, let me tell yawl, I love different colored bell peppers! It's the artist in me, so we are going to use three different colored bell peppers, red, green, and yellow. Wait until you taste these mouth-watering peppers. Follow the recipe closely and do it with love. This recipe makes a dozen peppers.

Ingredients:

Preheat your oven to 350°F.

1 quart of shrimp stock

6 large green bell peppers cut in half (for stuffing)

1 large yellow onion, chopped

3 stems of Italian parsley chopped

½ of a pound of claw or lump crabmeat

3 cloves of fresh garlic chopped

1 green bell pepper chopped

2 stems of green onions chopped

2 tablespoons of garlic powder

3 teaspoons creole seasoning

2 teaspoons of Old Bay Seasoning

1 pound of fresh peeled and deveined shrimp

2 tablespoons of olive oil

1 cup of Italian breadcrumbs

3 pieces of stale French bread

Directions:

Cut bell peppers in half. Straight down the middle is the way I like them. Remove the seeds and wash them with cold water. You can pre-boil your peppers for 3-5 minutes, or just put water at the bottom of your pan to soften peppers while cooking. In a large skillet, put olive oil in, then sautée all fresh seasoning, add shrimp, crabmeat, breadcrumbs, and French bread. Then add shrimp stock, powdered seasonings, garlic powder, creole seasoning, and Old Bay Seasoning. Mix well together to make the consistency like that similar to dressing. Make sure it's moist and not too dry. Now stuff your peppers and place them in the oven for 1 hour and 15 minutes. You can sprinkle a little breadcrumb on top and a little butter to keep it moist. Place foil over peppers. It serves 12. Enjoy!

Creole Orleans Mirliton Dressing

Oh, my God! This is a rare holiday favorite, and it will melt in your mouth. Now I will brag about my Aunt Connie Jordan. Her dressing was one of the best I have ever tasted. She would add lots of crabmeat and shrimp. It was moist and perfect. I realize that not too many folks in New Orleans like cooking it, unlike bell peppers. It really is a rare treat, and not too many restaurants serve it. The key is seafood and fresh seasoning. Baby! You've got to boil them things down for an hour or more to get them soft. Some folks say *casserole* or *stuffing*, but we say dressing in New Orleans!

Note: To make half a pan of dressing you will need about six large mirlitons. Boil for at least one hour and a half to soften. Drain the water. Please take the seeds out, and you can actually replant them!

Ingredients:

Preheat the oven to 375°F.

2 pounds of shrimp, peeled and deveined

2 large onions chopped

2 large green bell peppers chopped

1 pound of lump crabmeat

1 pound of claw crabmeat (optional)

½ stick of butter

2 tablespoons of olive oil

3 cloves of garlic chopped

3 stems of Italian parsley chopped

1 bowl of seafood stock

1 pound of your favorite sausage (I use beef or pork Hillshire Farm sausage.)

3 tablespoons of creole seasoning

3 tablespoons of seafood seasoning

2 teaspoons of garlic powder

1 tablespoon of Old Bay Seasoning

Directions:

In a pot, sautée your fresh seasoning, onion, bell pepper, garlic, and parsley with your olive oil and butter, and then add the shrimp and sausage. Mix in your softened, boiled down mirliton and breadcrumbs. Add powdered seasoning and mix very well. Place in a baking dish of your choice and cook uncovered for 1 hour and 15 minutes. When you see that beautiful brown crust on top, it will blow your mind, and the taste is divine. This serves 6. Enjoy!

Oyster Dressing

Whew, Lord! People don't like to fool with oysters, especially raw. In New Orleans, we use oysters and make so many dishes from them. You can eat them raw, with that good ole cocktail sauce on crackers, or fried just right. Not too hard or too soft. Oyster Po-Boy on French bread is a must when making a dressing, or as some call it, a casserole. Many restaurants have some type of oyster dish on the menu, especially raw oysters. They are often sold by the ½ dozen or dozen. But ironically, oyster dressing is rarely on the menu. My grandmother only cooked this dish a few times during my lifetime. Her oyster dressing was so moist. That is the way I like it, and love to cook it. So please don't knock it until you try it.

Use an 11x17 baking dish. You will need to have 1/2 loaf of French bread or 8 pieces of regular white bread for this recipe.

Ingredients:

Preheat oven to 350°F.

2 quarts of raw oysters

1 stick of butter

1 celery chopped

2 whole green bell peppers chopped

2 large onions chopped

6 cloves of garlic chopped

3 stems Fresh Italian parsley chopped

1 teaspoon of sage

1 teaspoon thyme

3 tablespoons of creole seasoning

2 tablespoons of garlic powder

1 tablespoon of onion powder

1 teaspoon of black pepper

Directions:

Cut your French bread or white bread up into small pieces and bake in the oven for 15 minutes until crispy and brown. Sautéé raw oysters in their juices to make a roux. Melt butter, and sautéé all of your fresh seasonings. It is especially important you don't skip the fresh seasoning, or your meal will just taste salty without them. Mix your celery, parsley, green bell peppers, and onions together. Add all of your powdered seasonings: thyme, creole seasoning, pepper, and sage. Now add your bread to your oysters and seasonings and mix well. Add to your baking dish and bake for one hour and a half. This recipe will make an unbeliever a believer in oysters. This feeds 6-8 people. Enjoy!

Seafood Cornbread Dressing (New Orleans Style)

You are probably thinking, do New Orleans natives change every traditional dish? Well, we are so creative and diverse; we love to add seafood to just about everything. Seafood dressing is another rare item, because it can be very expensive depending on the seafood you choose. The goal is not for it to taste like traditional cornbread dressing; we love being innovative in our culture and are not afraid to go against the norm. I love diversity. So, this recipe will make your mouth water like a river flowing, and you might not go back to just regular cornbread dressing. My husband loves this dish.

Note: You will need to boil your shrimp heads to make a shrimp stock to add to your dressing. Use the shrimp heads from the same fresh shrimp you used to put in the dressing. However, if you don't have access to fresh shrimp, then use seafood broth or chicken broth in a box or can. Do not use Jiffy Cornbread Mix. It will make your dish sweet.

Ingredients:

Preheat oven to 350°F.

2 quarts of shrimp stock or seafood broth

2 stalks of celery

Use your favorite cornbread mix (I use Martha White Cornbread Mix.)

1 pound of lump crabmeat

2 pounds of raw shrimp, cleaned and deveined

5 stems of Italian parsley chopped

2 large yellow onions chopped

2 large green bell peppers chopped

1 large red bell pepper chopped

3 cloves of garlic chopped

2 crushed bay leaves (Boil with the seafood stock.)

1 stick of butter

3 tablespoons of seafood seasoning

2 tablespoons of Old Bay Seasoning

1 tablespoon of creole seasoning

1 box of Italian breadcrumbs (You can also use baked French bread.)

Directions:

Once you have finished baking your cornbread and it has cooled down, mash up cornbread (also tear up French bread if that is what you are using). Mix the cornbread with the breadcrumbs (French bread) together. Add shrimp stock. Sautée the onion, bell pepper, garlic, and celery in olive oil and butter, then add shrimp and crab meat. Add the cornbread and mix well until moist. You don't want to have it too dry. If you think it is too dry, just add some water or more chicken or shrimp broth. Butter the bottom of your pan, and place dressing in it. Bake for 1 hour and 15 minutes. Serve 10 - 15. Enjoy!

Festival Crawfish Bread

Oh my God, my supporters and customers love this popular item. Most of the time, you would only get this at New Orleans festivals, such as Jazz Fest, French Quarter Festival, or Gentilly Fest. That is why I am calling this Festival Crawfish Bread. I don't know who the original creator of this dish is, but it is so New Orleans. Boiled crawfish brings together many families. Why do we love these little mud bugs so much? Boiled crawfish, potatoes, corn, smoked sausage, shrimp, and crabs are a real Seafood Boil, and sometimes your mouth will be on fire. So, the crawfish tails from the boiled crawfish are used for this dish. You can peel them yourself if you have access to boiled crawfish or buy them prepackaged. You will be amazed at how simple and easy this recipe is. The importance of having Louisiana crawfish tails is that it will give it the authentic taste you desire. So, when buying them at your local grocery stores, look for that. However, some states may not even carry crawfish tails.

Ingredients:

Preheat oven to 325°F.
2 packs of Louisiana cooked crawfish or peeled crawfish tails
1 stick of salted butter
1 pack of Gouda cheese
1 pack of sharp cheddar cheese
1 large yellow onion
1 large red bell pepper
1 large green bell pepper
4 cloves of fresh garlic
4 stems of fresh Italian parsley
1 tablespoon of mayonnaise
2 loaves of French bread
1 teaspoon of garlic powder
2 tablespoons of Tony Chachere's Creole seasoning

Directions:

Sautéé the onion, green and red bell pepper, garlic, and parsley in butter, and olive oil with the crawfish tails for about 20 minutes until the tails are tender. Then add your gouda and cheddar cheese and stir it continually. Turn off the fire on your stove, let it cool down for 5 minutes, and then add mayonnaise. Cut your French bread into anywhere from 3 to 6-inch squares and spread crawfish sauce on top. Place in oven for 10 minutes. Serves 12. Enjoy this amazing treat.

Stick to your Bones
Southern Recipes

Monday Red Beans and Rice

Now let me tell you, my grandmother's red beans and rice was the undermining of a straight fool. It would have you going for seconds, thirds, and later for fourths after the deep nap you would have to take, because of the food coma that results from its awesomeness. I remember her soaking those beans for a few hours and sometimes as long as a day. This process speeds up cooking time and makes the beans easier to digest. It gets rid of the phytic acid and phytohemagglutinin in the beans, plus they cream better. It is a grand tradition in Louisiana, especially in New Orleans. We have a deep love for red beans, and most households, restaurants, and chefs serve it on Mondays or have it on the menu. You would be surprised at how many of us grew up eating this dish, and how many children love it. My grandmother made the creamiest red beans ever. Follow my recipe, and you will be in love with red beans forever.

Note: The key to creamy red beans is soaking them for at least 6-8 hours. I usually do 24 hours. My grandmother would add cooking oil to her beans, and in this recipe, I do the same. The best type of red beans is Camellia red kidney beans. If they are not sold in your state, just use red kidney beans.

Ingredients:

1-pound red kidney beans
2 large yellow onions chopped
2 large green bell peppers chopped
6 cloves of garlic chopped
2 stems of Italian parsley chopped
6 bay leaves
2 teaspoons of crushed red pepper
4 stems of green onions chopped
1 red bell pepper (optional)
3 tablespoons of creole seasoning
3 tablespoons of garlic powder
1 teaspoon of sage
1 teaspoon of salt
2 pounds of smoked sausage pork, beef, or turkey (Whatever is your preference.)
2 smoked ham hocks for taste
1 pound of pickled pork is optional (must boil down to get salt out first)

Directions:

Rinse your soaked beans and fill a large pot halfway with water. Add all your raw fresh seasonings, powdered seasoning, 2 tablespoons of cooking oil, ½ stick of butter, bay leaves, beans, and meat. Cook for at least 2-3 hours on top of the stove. Serves 10-12 people. Enjoy over rice.

Turkey Wings and Gravy

Oh boy, another dish I love so much that my grandmother cooked. Her gravy was so thick, you could just eat it with rice and be full. I don't know why the turkey wing skin with a little fat was so enjoyable to me. The wings are the best part. But you must cook them long enough so they will be tender. Some folks who hated cooking whole turkeys for the holidays would use this shortcut method with some dressing. My grandmother did both. She would have at least two turkeys and turkey wings. Baby, my grandmother Lois had the best. But this is my recipe that you will enjoy. The key is tenderness, because you are going to bake them first and then cook them down.

Ingredients:

Preheat oven to 375°F.

6 total pieces of turkey wings and drumsticks

1 green bell pepper chopped

1 yellow onion chopped

3 cloves of garlic chopped

1 quart of chicken stock

2 bay leaves

1 teaspoon of crushed pepper

1 teaspoon of pepper

2 teaspoons of salt

3 tablespoons of creole seasoning

2 tablespoons of Kitchen Bouquet

½ of flour

1 tablespoon of cornstarch

Directions:

Use a 10-quart stockpot. Season your turkey meat with your powdered creole seasoning and place it in the oven uncovered for one hour. In your stock pot, sautée your fresh seasoning, bell pepper, onion, and garlic for 3 minutes. Pour in chicken stock and add 2 tablespoons of Kitchen Bouquet. Once the turkey wings are done in the oven, place them in a pot and boil on medium heat for an hour. Add cornstarch to thicken your gravy and serve over rice. Serves 4. Enjoy!

Creamy Chicken Pasta

My son loves my Chicken Pasta. It is a blessing that chicken can be used for multiple recipes, and they all taste different. This dish was not popular in my family overall, but in my household, we use it a lot. Especially after I started the catering business. Seafood Pasta is the traditional pasta of choice in New Orleans, but Chicken Pasta is becoming more popular than ever, and it is so filling that you don't need any sides to go with it. I love to cook this dish, especially for the children. Everyone doesn't eat seafood or may be allergic to shellfish, so this is an alternative. This recipe is for half of a pan.

Ingredients:

1 whole baked chicken cut or cooked leg quarters cut up
2 packs of fettuccine or penne pasta
3 cloves of garlic chopped
1 green bell pepper chopped
1 yellow onion chopped
1 red bell pepper chopped
1 small can of cream of mushroom soup
2 stems of curly parsley chopped
4 oz. of whipping cream
1 tablespoon of olive oil
1 stick of salted butter
3 tablespoons of chicken seasoning
3 tablespoons of creole seasoning

Directions:

Boil your pasta in a 10-quart stock pot, drain, and place it to the side. In a large saucepan, sauté garlic, bell pepper, and onions with olive oil. Add cut-up chicken, chicken broth, cream of mushroom soup, and whipping cream. Cook on medium heat for about 20 minutes. Place the cooked fettuccine in half a pan, pour your sauce over the pasta, and mix well. Serves 8. Enjoy!

Creole Creamy Shrimp Pasta

This is definitely a favorite New Orleans dish. Almost every party menu will have this dish on it. At every party or wedding event we attended, shrimp pasta was on the menu. We love some pasta dishes in New Orleans. But you must be careful when using cream and seafood together. It can spoil you if it is not in the right setting or left out too long unattended. I have several recipes for shrimp pasta, but I want to share this one with you. New Orleans folk will use any and every kind of pasta noodles to make this dish, including spaghetti. But you can also use penne, fettuccine, angel hair, etc. For this recipe, we will use penne pasta. This recipe will make half of a pan.

Ingredients:

3 bags of penne or fettuccine pasta

2 pounds of freshly cleaned and deveined shrimp (You can use frozen shrimp as well, but it takes longer to soften.)

6 cloves of garlic

1 whole stalk of green onion chopped

1 yellow onion chopped

1 green bell pepper chopped

1 red bell pepper chopped

1 yellow bell pepper chopped

4 stems of Italian parsley chopped

3 tablespoons of powdered seafood seasoning

2 tablespoons of garlic powder

2 tablespoons of creole seasoning

2 teaspoons of Accent

1 stick of butter

1 half of a carton of whipping cream

1 tablespoon of evaporated milk

3 tablespoons of parmesan cheese (optional)

Directions:

Boil your pasta and place it to the side. Sautéé fresh seasoning, garlic, onion and green, red, and yellow bell peppers, and parsley. Add shrimp, butter, and whipping cream. Put your seasonings in the mix. Add Parmesan cheese to thicken. Mix in your penne pasta. Sprinkle with dry parsley flakes for decoration and serving. Serves 10. Enjoy!

Southern Cheesy Baked Macaroni

Again, oh boy. This dish will always be a favorite for children and adults, no matter what state you live in. My grandmother also mastered this dish as well. She always cooked this. Especially on holidays and Sundays, sometimes with a pot roast, yams, and peas. This is the cheesiest macaroni ever. She would always say that the Government commodity cheese was the best. This recipe is going to blow your mind because of how cheesy and moist it is. This side dish can go with anything. The key is using real cheese, and not processed. This recipe makes a half pan.

Ingredients:

Preheat oven to 350°F.
2 packs of elbow macaroni
1 stick of salted butter
1 can of evaporated milk
½ can of Half and Half
2 oz. bag of Gouda cheese
3 oz. bag of sharp cheddar cheese
1/3 cup of olive oil
3 teaspoons of salt
1 tablespoon of pepper
2 stems of fresh cut parsley

Directions:

Boil your elbow macaroni and drain the water in a strainer. Place cooked macaroni back in the pot, and add evaporated milk, butter and half and half. Add salt, pepper, and creole seasoning. Add half of the Gouda cheese and half of the cheddar cheese. Mix well until butter and cheese are melted. It should be cheesy. Add to your greased baking pan and place the rest of your cheese on top with chopped parsley. Pour olive oil on top and cook uncovered for 45 minutes until you see that crispy beautiful brown top. Serves 10. Enjoy!

Tasteful and Delightful Recipes

Green Onion Mashed Potatoes

This simple recipe will make you smile. The green onions create a burst of flavor with your potatoes, and it's easy on the eyes. Green onions are a powerful fresh seasoning. I love to cook with them. The key is fresh potatoes.

Ingredients:

3 stems of green onions chopped really fine
1/3 of a cup of olive oil
5 potatoes
6 cloves of garlic chopped
1 ½ sticks of salted butter
Salt and pepper to taste
1 stem of fresh Italian parsley chopped

Directions:

In a large pot, boil your potatoes down until softened. Peel potatoes and mash them. Sauté garlic with olive oil and parsley. Add to potatoes with butter, salt, and pepper. Mix well and add the green onions. Serves 6. Enjoy!

Creamy Creole Potato Salad

There is a common saying that is often asked at a function. "Who made the potato salad?" It is a serious taboo if you make bad potato salad in our culture. Now I must admit, my grandmother's potato salad was good, but not the best. For some strange reason, she loved to put orange food coloring in it, to make it look orange. It was well-seasoned too. I hear horror stories of people making the worse potato salad, even putting raisins in it. Oh my God! But you will love mine, and let me tell you, most of my elders who have eaten my potato salad highly approve. So let me break it down for you.

Ingredients:

6 golden potatoes

6 eggs

2 stems of Italian parsley chopped

2 stems of green onions

1 red bell pepper

1 green bell pepper

1 yellow onion

2 teaspoons of pepper

2 tablespoons of creole seasoning

½ cup of mayonnaise

¼ cup of olive oil

Directions:

Boil eggs and potatoes in a large pot. Add salt so the shells of the eggs will come off easily. Cut up all your fresh seasoning fine. Peel the eggs and separate the yolks from the whites. Peel the potatoes and mash them. Add all your cut up seasoning, your cut up boiled egg whites, mayonnaise, and then add creole seasoning and pepper. Mix well. Lastly add the yellow smashed egg yolks. Mix well until creamy. Add a little olive oil and place the potato salad in the fridge to cool. Serves 10. Enjoy!

Shrimp with Homemade Spaghetti Sauce (New Orleans Way)

Ok, I know you are laughing and saying, "Who told you to change this Italian dish to a New Orleans Dish?" Some people do not eat red meat but love the red sauce. So, think of this as a substitute for the pescatarians. We cannot leave them out, right? But once you taste it, you will fall madly in love with it. You will thank me later. My husband and I both love to cook, but I am not a fan of red sauce, he is. I remember going on a meat fast and I used shrimp for this dish. I also cooked this for a guest on my cooking show, "Cooking with Love." She loved the dish, and you will too!

Ingredients:

1 dozen ripe tomatoes
1 pack of angel hair or thin spaghetti
1 yellow onion chopped
1 red bell pepper chopped
2 large green bell peppers chopped
4 stalks of green onions chopped
4 stems of Italian parsley chopped
1 stem from curly parsley chopped
3 cloves of garlic chopped
2 tablespoons of garlic powder
3 tablespoons of garlic and herbs seasoning
2 teaspoons of sage
1 stem of thyme
1 teaspoon of crushed red pepper
3 tablespoons of creole seasoning
1 tablespoon of basil
3 bay leaves
2 tablespoons of olive oil
2 teaspoons of raw sugar
1 teaspoon of salt
2 teaspoons of pepper
2 dozen fresh, clean, and deveined shrimp (You can also use frozen shrimp.)

Directions:

Dice and slice the fresh tomatoes, mash them up, or use a food processor for your sauce. Sauté all your fresh seasonings: bell peppers (green and red), garlic, parsley, green onion, and yellow onion for about 5 minutes with your shrimp in olive oil. Then add to your tomato sauce. Cook for 45 minutes and serve over angel hair pasta or thin spaghetti. Serves 8. Enjoy!

Southern Smothered Chicken

Now, if you can go back in time and remember this dish from our elders, you will appreciate this recipe. It is so simple, yet so filling. Chicken is such a universal dish and can be cooked a thousand ways. This is not just a New Orleans favorite, but a Southern dish. When you think of smothered chicken, you think of Sunday dinner with some yams and cornbread. I am getting hungry just thinking about it. I had three grandmothers in my lifetime and a great-grandmother whom I was blessed to be around. My biological father's mother, Mae Duplessis, was also a superb cook and came from a large family. She had 11 children. I used to visit with my sister. She knew we loved to eat, and I remember this dish cooked by her and it was so delicious and tender.

Ingredients:

1 bag of leg quarters (Cut them in half.)
4 chicken breasts (Boneless or bone-in.)
2 large yellow onions chopped
1 large orange bell pepper chopped
1 large red bell pepper chopped
2 cloves of garlic chopped
2 stems of green onions chopped
2 stems of Italian parsley chopped
2 tablespoons of parsley flakes
2 tablespoons of onion powder
2 tablespoons of chicken seasoning
3 tablespoons of cornstarch
1 tablespoon of unbleached flour
1 teaspoon of Kitchen Bouquet

Directions:

Fill your stew pot up halfway with water and add raw chicken. Add all your fresh seasonings: yellow onions, green, red, and orange bell peppers, garlic, and green onions. Add your powdered seasonings and a teaspoon of Kitchen Bouquet. Bring to a boil on medium heat for 1 hour, and then add your cornstarch and flour to thicken it. Stir well. Cook for 10 more, and the gravy will taste like it came from Heaven. Serves 10. Enjoy!

Sauté Creole Catfish

This is one of the easiest recipes you can fix in a short amount of time. Catfish are cooked in so many ways in New Orleans, especially with cream sauces on top. But this is just a simple way to cook your catfish. I love to eat this with sautéed veggies and angel hair pasta. But you must get real catfish, and not that Swai fish that looks similar to catfish. Unfortunately, many people will pass this off as catfish. Wild-caught catfish are the best tasting fresh fish. But farmed raised is fine too. I remember cooking this dish on my cooking show for a local pastor who is also a baker. He was amazed at how easy this dish was to make and how delicious it was.

Ingredients:

5 ounces of fresh wild-caught catfish
½ stick of butter
4 cloves of garlic chopped
3 stems of fresh Italian parsley chopped
1 red bell pepper chopped
1 green bell pepper chopped
3 teaspoons of garlic powder
3 tablespoons of creole seasoning
1 tablespoon of Old Bay Seasoning
3 tablespoons of olive oil

Directions:

Season your catfish with your powdered seasonings: garlic powder, creole seasoning, and Old Bay Seasoning. Place butter and olive oil in a frying pan. Sauté fresh seasoning, garlic, red and green bell peppers, and parsley for 3 minutes, then add the catfish. Each side should cook for 5 minutes until tender. Serve alone or over angel hair and veggies. This is a lovely light meal that serves 2—4. Enjoy!

Shrimp Eggplant Medley

This is a simple, delicious, and light dish. You can do so much with eggplant, and adding the shrimp will blow your mind. It is light and tasty. Eggplant is a New Orleans favorite. You can even make a dressing with it. But let's show you step by step how to create this healthy Southern dish. My husband and I were playing in the kitchen one day. He loves to use leeks just like the chefs in the Chinese culture do, but this recipe has squash added, and it gave it a burst. Eggplant can be fried or grilled, and it is so healthy and delicious. I put this on my website as a dish to sell, and people love it.

Ingredients:

2 large eggplants
1 large yellow squash
1 pound of shrimp, cleaned and deveined
1 yellow bell pepper finely chopped
1 red bell pepper finely chopped
1 green bell pepper finely chopped
1 clove of garlic finely chopped
3 tablespoons of garlic and herbs powdered seasoning
1 tablespoon of seafood seasoning
1 teaspoon of garlic powder
3 tablespoons olive oil

Directions:

Dice and cut up eggplant and squash to the equivalent size of a quarter. Pour two tablespoons of olive oil into a saucepan on medium heat. Add eggplant, squash, shrimp, fresh seasoning, red, yellow, and green bell pepper, and sprinkle on powdered seasoning: garlic and herbs, garlic powder, and seafood seasoning. Sauté for 15 minutes. Serves 6. Enjoy!

Jaw-dropping Soups, Gumbo, Fish

Drunken Soup

Okay, now this jewel of a dish comes from my husband. Some years back, my mother-in-law's friend was sick in the hospital, and he hated the food. So, my husband made this soup and sent it to him. Behold, the man said he felt so much better after eating it. It is so hearty and unbelievable, you won't taste the wine, but it's in there. A good soup is excellent for the soul. This tasty, yet simple dish soothes the soul. It has White Zinfandel in it. Yum, yum!

Ingredients:

2 quarts of White Zinfandel
1 quart of chicken stock
1 large cabbage chopped
2 yellow onions chopped
2 red onions chopped
1 green bell pepper chopped
1 red bell pepper chopped
1 yellow bell pepper chopped
1 orange bell pepper chopped
5 cloves of garlic chopped
2 tablespoons of creole seasoning
2 tablespoons of Tony Chachere's Seasoning
1 teaspoon of garlic powder
1 bay leaf

Directions:

Place diced cabbage in a soup pot and add cut up seasoning: yellow and red onions, green, red, yellow, and orange bell peppers, garlic, and bay leaf. Then add your powdered seasoning. Simmer on the stove on medium heat for an hour and 15 minutes. Serves 8 -10. Enjoy!

Crabmeat and Shrimp Soup

This recipe belongs to my husband. He has always loved to place cream of chicken and cream of mushroom soup in his recipes. He told me his late father used it a lot as well. The first time we sold this dish was back in November 2020 and it was a hit. Our customers go crazy about this delicious dish. It is quite simple and quick. Perfect for the Fall and Winter months. But you can cook it anytime you feel like it. Just imagine sitting by the fire, or by the Christmas tree eating this on a cold winter night, it's perfect.

Ingredients:

1 6oz can of cream of chicken soup
1 6oz of cream of mushroom soup
½ pound of shrimp
½ pound of lump crabmeat
1 red bell pepper chopped
1 green pepper chopped
2 stems of fresh Italian parsley chopped
3 cloves of garlic chopped
2 teaspoons of paprika
1 teaspoon of creole seasoning
1 cup of shrimp stock (or water with 1 teaspoon of crab boil)
½ stick of butter
1/3 tablespoon of olive oil

Directions:

Place all fresh seasoning in a medium soup pot: bell peppers red and green, parsley, and garlic, and sautée for 3 minutes. Add in the cream of mushroom soup and cream of chicken soup. Sprinkle in your seasonings: paprika and creole seasoning after adding in shrimp stock. Add butter and olive oil. Cook on medium heat for 20 minutes. Add shrimp and crab meat and cook for another 10 minutes. Your meal will be ready in 30 minutes. Serves 8. Enjoy!

Tomato Basil Soup

If you love red sauces and especially tomatoes, then you will love this recipe. I suggest you use fresh tomatoes and not canned ones. You can always tell the difference. This simple soup will fill you up. It's very light and hearty.

Ingredients:

2 pounds of ripe plum tomatoes
2 yellow onions chopped
3 cloves of garlic chopped
2 cups of fresh basil leaves
1 green bell pepper chopped
1 tablespoon of unsalted butter
1 teaspoon of raw sugar (non-bleached)
1 small can of tomatoes
1 teaspoon of sea salt
½ quart of chicken stock

Directions:

Dice up and puree your tomatoes in a 6-quart stockpot over medium heat. Sautéé bell pepper, onions, and garlic with butter and olive oil for 7 minutes. Add pureed tomatoes, basil, and chicken stock. Add salt and sugar. Cook on medium heat and let it simmer for 30 minutes uncovered. Serves 6. Enjoy!

Creole Okra Gumbo

When you think of Louisiana cuisine, you must include okra. Okra was first introduced by African slaves in the 18th century as a thickening roux for gumbo and has been here ever since. New Orleans has a great love for okra, and it is healthy for you. I was even taught that the slime in the okra (that many hate) is good for your stomach as a natural remedy for indigestion. My grandmother used okra also to thicken her gumbo. When I started cooking Okra Gumbo, people went crazy, and it is in high demand. I cook it with love and people are in love with it. I use fresh okra often to make this dish, but if you don't have access, you can use frozen. You can make this gumbo with or without a roux. I have a Dry Gumbo Roux that I created, and I use it from time to time on this recipe. But the okra is already thick. If you would rather have the brown colored gumbo instead of the light green with a hint of red, then make your roux.

Ingredients:

3 pounds of fresh okra cut and diced

3 pounds fresh or frozen shrimp peeled and deveined, (Save shrimp heads for your stock.)

2 pounds of beef, andouille, or pork sausage

2 large red bell peppers chopped

2 large green bell peppers chopped

6 cloves of garlic chopped

1 large yellow onion chopped

1 pound of lump crabmeat

2 tablespoons of tomato paste

2 teaspoons of crushed red pepper

2 stalks of celery chopped

6 bay leaves

3 tablespoons of creole seasoning

3 tablespoons of Old Bay Seasoning

2 teaspoons of garlic powder

½ cup of Vinegar or 1/3 cup of cooking oil (To precook slime out of okra.)

Directions:

In a large stockpot, cook your shrimp heads to make stock for your gumbo. Boil for about 15 minutes, take shrimp heads out, and place to the side. In a pot precook okra with vinegar to take some of the slime out for about 7 minutes, stirring continually. Sautée sausage, onion, celery, bell peppers, and garlic. Pour into a stock pot with shrimp stock, add okra, bay leaves, crushed pepper, and tomato paste. Cook on medium heat for an hour and then add shrimp and crabmeat. Serve over rice. Serves 20 - 30. Enjoy!

Dry Gumbo Roux Mix

This is not a recipe, but one of my creations I want to share with you. The Gumbo Roux is the most important base of your gumbo. It takes time, patience, and love to create that perfect brown peanut butter-colored roux. Depending on how big your pot of gumbo will be, it could take up to an hour or more. Some folks dread this process because if you burn it, you must start over and throw the burnt roux away. Roux is comprised of flour and cooking oil, and you must be consistent when stirring it on the stove. One day, I was just thinking about a creative way to make great gumbo, and the Dry Gumbo Roux idea was born in late 2020. I experimented with it for almost a year until I finally had the right ingredients to pull it all together. It's a perfect blend of herbs and spices with no salt or oil. "Make your gumbo life easier," is my slogan.

This Dry Gumbo Roux is magical, and I have had rave reviews from so many locals and people from across the world. Even first-time gumbo makers have success stories. This dry roux cuts your time in half, and it renders a burst of delicious flavor. It's still in its grassroots stages and soon will be in grocery stores. The packets are 4 ounces, and you can cook at least 1 to 2 quarts of gumbo with it. I also include suggestions and instructions on the packets.

For more info about ordering and shipping, contact us at the drygumboroux.com website or our email address, dryrouxgumbo@gmail.com.

Creole Crispy New Orleans Catfish

This Southern delight is served in most restaurants in New Orleans. It's a favorite, especially when it's fresh Louisiana wild-caught catfish. My clients and customers love the way I fry my catfish. I often try to use fresh farm-raised or wild-caught, but I use frozen as well. So, whatever you can use or have access to, please do so. Catfish is also used for Po-Boys or aka poor-boys on French bread. Almost every corner store sells this, or catfish plates with fries. I know, right; we put everything on French bread. Some menus and restaurants will call this a seafood platter, and it will include catfish, shrimp, hush puppies, fried oysters, etc. I have sold platters before and it's a winner. But I remember my elders cooking pan-fried catfish in a cast-iron skillet with old regular corn meal, no fish fry, just cornmeal. Something about it brings back so many memories.

Ingredients:

4 (4 oz) pieces of catfish
2 cups old-fashioned cornmeal
Zatarain's Fish Fry
1 egg
1/2 cup of dry parsley flakes
1 lemon
2 cups canola oil
3 tablespoons of creole seasoning
2 teaspoons of pepper

Directions:

Pour canola oil into a 14-inch frying pan, preferably cast iron, which can take up to four pieces of fish at one time. In a bowl, beat your eggs and lightly season catfish with your creole seasoning. In a ziplock bag mix old fashion corn meal and Zatarain's Fish Fry, add parsley flakes, pepper, and a little creole seasoning. Remember you have already seasoned the fish, and you don't want it to be too salty. Dip the catfish in your egg mix and then place it in the ziplock bag with the batter. Shake well until the cornmeal mix is covering the entire fish on both sides. Put oil on high heat, wait 5 minutes, and place fish in the hot oil. Each side should be cooked for 5 minutes. If you have a deep fryer, it will take less time. I recommend serving some good old-fashioned potato salad and corn with the fish, and a piece of garlic bread. Serves 4. Enjoy!

Vegan Eggplant Medley

After the pandemic, a friend of mine introduced me to vegan meals and I fell in love with them. I did a fast on those meals and lost a bunch of weight. I never realized how tasty and delicious vegan foods were. This motivated me to cook vegan meals for my customers in 2020. This is a vegan or vegetarian dish, and it's a favorite. Yes, we have many people from all walks of life living in New Orleans who don't eat meat or seafood. But there are so many vegetable dishes that taste just as well, and it is all about using fresh seasoning and herbs.

Ingredients:

2 large eggplants chopped
1 large squash chopped
3 stalks of carrots chopped
1 green bell pepper chopped
1 red bell pepper chopped
4 cloves of garlic minced
3 tablespoons of garlic and herbs
1 teaspoon of sea salt
1/3 of olive oil

Directions:

In a 10-inch saucepan, place eggplants, squash, carrots, bell peppers, and garlic. Add garlic and herbs, seasoning, and sautéé down with olive oil for 15 minutes. Great as a side dish. Serves 6. Enjoy!

Mouth Watering Desserts

Honey Molasses Grilled Apples

This tasty dessert happened by a fluke. I wanted something sweet but healthy, and I had some apples that I did not want to go bad and had some molasses in the cabinet. I put it on my menu one day and a friend of mine bought it and loved it. Molasses is magical to me, they can wake up anything, especially desserts. This recipe is so simple and delicious.

Ingredients:

2 red apples (Cut into fours.)
1/3 of raw sugar (unbleached)
2 tablespoons of condensed milk
2 tablespoons of butter (unsalted)
3 tablespoons of raw unfiltered honey
3 tablespoons of molasses

Directions:

In a medium-sized skillet, grease the skillet with some butter, pour in sliced apples, and add raw sugar and butter. Sautéé for 2 minutes and then add condensed milk and honey. Sautéé until the apples are slightly soft. Then add molasses and cook down for 5 minutes. Eat hot but can be eaten cold. Pour over vanilla ice cream if you like. Makes 8 servings. Enjoy!

Southern Orleans Carrot Soufflée

Let me tell you, growing up, we went to many places to eat. Piccadilly was a favorite, because of their Carrot Soufflée. I have learned that so many people never had it or turn their nose up at it because they hate carrots. The funny part is, you won't even taste the bitter carrots, because of the ingredients used. To me, it tastes more like it's in the sweet potato family. I cook my own and I absolutely love Carrot Soufflée. It is one of my favorite dishes. Who would have thought carrots could make such a pleasurable dessert? This recipe is simple and delicious. You will also need a mixer.

Ingredients:

Preheat the oven to 350°F.
2 pounds of carrots peeled and chopped
½ cup of raw sugar (unbleached)
2 teaspoons of pure vanilla extract
3 eggs beaten
½ stick of butter melted
1 tablespoon of condensed milk
1 teaspoon of unbleached flour
1 teaspoon of baking powder
2 tablespoons of powdered sugar to sprinkle on top

Directions:

Boil peeled and chopped carrots in a pot until softened, and then place them in a bowl. Add eggs, sugar, condensed milk, flour, baking powder, vanilla extract, and melted butter. Mix well with your mixer until smooth. Make sure there are no lumps. Make sure your ingredients are well blended. Pour into a greased baking pan and cook for one hour. Once it is cooled down, sprinkle your powdered sugar on top and serve. Serves about 8 people. Enjoy!

Amaretto Pecan Bread Pudding with Sauce

Now, truth be told, this is one bread pudding recipe I will share out of many, and this one is tasteful and delicious. For most of our family functions, I always cook this bread pudding, and people always rave about it. Once you try this, you won't want to go back to just using regular bread. Bread pudding is actually at the top of my list of favorite desserts. When I see bread pudding on the menu, I will order it. It doesn't matter what other dessert is on there. You can create all kinds of bread pudding with or without raisins. The rum sauce is an added treat to any bread pudding. I love to eat it warm with vanilla ice cream. You will need to use a mixer when creating this recipe.

Ingredients:

Preheat oven to 350°F.

2 loaves of stale French bread cut into cubes

3 eggs beaten

1 stick of butter

1 cup of raw sugar (unbleached)

1 teaspoon of ground cinnamon

2 cups of milk

½ of raisins

½ of pecans

1 tablespoon of condensed milk

For the Amaretto Sauce

4 tablespoons of Amaretto

2 tablespoons of butter

1 cup of evaporated milk

1 tablespoon of cornstarch

½ cup of raw sugar (unbleached)

Directions:

In a mixing bowl, place cut-up French bread, pour milk in, and mix well. Add eggs, butter, sugar, ground cinnamon, and condensed milk. Mix well together, then add raisins and pecans. Pour into greased baking pan and place in the oven uncovered for one hour. In a saucepan pour in the Amaretto liquor, butter, evaporated milk, and raw sugar. Cook on medium heat for 5 minutes and then add cornstarch to thicken. Once the bread pudding is done, pour Amaretto sauce over the bread pudding. Serves 10 people. Enjoy!

About The Author

Trinese Jordan Duplessis was born and raised in New Orleans, Louisiana. Trinese is a great visionary and entrepreneur who have multiple gifts and talents that keep growing. She is a wife, mother, an award-winning playwright, director, actress, TV and radio personality, poet, host, motivational speaker, and Chef. She is the owner of Oritri Catering Company. Trinese uses her ministry as a platform who has helped many people, artist, actors and supporters throughout the United States. Trinese has a following from Ghana, Africa, China, Japan. She knows God has called her to be a leader. She is also the CEO and Co-owner of T. Duplessis Entertainment LLC, created in 2011 with her husband. She credits her husband as her backbone and biggest supporter.

Trinese has been writing since a young child, she says her family is full of characters, and she owes her comedic gifts to her late Grandfather. Trinese wrote her first stage play for her church back in 2008 titled, "Saving Justin" and since she has been non-stop, writing, producing and directing. T. Duplessis Entertainment LLC is more than just entertainment; it is a movement, and a ministry. Trinese stepped out of faith and obeyed instructions from God to build a legacy/ brand through drama outside the four walls of the church, after doing several stage plays, performances, monologues, and skits.

Trinese Duplessis has written and directed at least 11 original stage plays, and has as many as 30 unpublished plays, a screen play, short films, movie, and books of poetry and short stories. But she never thought her first published book would be a cookbook, specifically this cookbook; but it would only make sense, because she come from a large family of chefs and cooks, and her Grandmother Lois Finley taught her early on, as young as 3 years old. Her love for great food is a part of her artistry.

In 2014, Trinese attended the DPI Playwrights Ball in New York and won Best Comedy of a Stage Play of the Year for "Light of the Ghetto", Starring Trinese Duplessis as Mama Tee. She also was nominated for Best Actress of the Year Award in 2020. She also worked on the set of Tyler Perry's Madea Farewell Tour. Trinese has worked on the sets of NCIS New Orleans, Queen Sugar, Claws, Girls Trip as a background actress.

Trinese has been featured in magazines locally to New Orleans including "A Dynasty of Dreamers" in 2017 and in 2018, "Upwords" based in India. Trinese has hosted several self-produced entertainment shows with musicians, actors, comedians, poets. She also hosted a comedy show at the famous Improv comedy club in Houston Tx, in 2018 for internet viral star Ms. Shirleen, and recently another Ms. Shirleen show at Café Istanbul in 2020. Trinese has a Local TV Show, *The Trinese Duplessis Show* that airs on Cox 76 every Friday 9am, Sundays 11:30am and 11:30pm CST.

She has written and produced of her own show since 2017. She co-hosted and produced an earlier show, "Hope for Today" for an 8-year period. Trinese has been in Television for a total of 13 years. Over eleven years in the entertainment business, and 5 years in the culinary industry. It has been bittersweet for the company with ups, and downs yet extremely rewarding at best.

T. Duplessis Entertainment LLC have helped, hired, and produced many artists, actors, actresses, musicians, comedians, and other producers and directors.

Trinese response, "We have built a great name for our Companies, and we are going Global at this rate." Trinese believes in building with integrity and character, and the sky is unlimited.

In "Tears on My Windowpane" Written and Directed by Trinese, she also plays the Role of Mama Tee, and Tamika. Trinese has been writing since she was a child, she recognized she had the gift in high school. She wrote her first Play in 2008, "Saving Justin", and a series of skits, monologues, poems etc. She was the Director of the Drama Department at her Church, post Hurricane Katrina from 2009-2012.

Her first Dinner Play, "Let's Stay Together was a sellout. Her stage credits include, "Delusion Versus Truth" in 2012. The Award-winning Stage Play "Light of the Ghetto" with Mama tee in 2012. Best comedy Stage Play of the Year. DPI Playwright's Awards gala, held in New York. "The Evil Mistress" in 2013, "God's Tears on my Windowpane" 2014." Light of the Ghetto II" 2015, "Mama Tee's Christmas" 2016 "Sweet Willie's Cotton Club 2017 and Part 2 of "God's Tears on my Windowpane"2018. "Chalkboard Bullying" Stage Play in 2019. She wrote her first short film, "The Corona Blues" in 2020, and her latest "There is a shortage in Heaven" in 2023.

For more information and to stay connected to Trinese Duplessis,

Catering website: oritricatering.org
Social Media:
https//www.instagram.com/oritricatering
www.twitter.com/lady73
www.facebook.com/trinese.duplessis1 and www.facebook.com/TduplessisEntertainment
https://www.facebook.com/trineseduplessis2/
https://www.facebook.com/trineseduplessisshow/.
https://www.facebook.com/The-Concrete-Bed-933767416766247/
https://www.facebook.com/PACO-the-ACTOR-105884207453962/
https://www.facebook.com/Sweet-Willies-Cotton-Club-Musical…/
https://www.instagram.com/tlovelyqueen/
https://www.instagram.com/trinesed/
https://www.instagram.com/sweetwilliesmusicalstageplay/
https://www.instagram.com/pacotheactor/?hl=en
https://www.instagram.com/thetrinese/?hl=en
https://www.facebook.com/mama.tjd/?fref=ts
www.youtube.com/user/tjdupless